THE
MOON
ISAAC ASIMOV

Illustrated by Alex Ebel

Follett Publishing Company   Chicago • New York

Copyright© 1966, by Follett Publishing Company. All rights reserved. No part of this book may be reproduced in any form without written permission from the publisher. Manufactured in the United States of America. Published simultaneously in Canada by The Ryerson Press, Toronto.

Library of Congress Catalog Card Number: AC 66-10622

SBN   695-45875-2   Titan binding   SBN   695-85875-0   Trade binding   Second Printing

NORTH

SEA OF COLD

PLATO

SEA OF HUMBOLDT

JURA MOUNTAINS

ALPS MOUNTAINS

LAKE OF SLEEPERS

ARCHIMEDES

HERODOTUS

SEA OF SHOWERS

SEA OF SERENITY

OCEAN OF STORMS

APENNINE MOUNTAINS

SEA OF CRISES

KEPLER

COPERNICUS

SEA OF VAPORS

GRIMALDI

SEA OF TRANQUILLITY

SEA OF FERTILITY

PTOLEMAEUS

LANGRENUS

SEA OF CLOUDS

ALTAI MOUNTAINS

SEA OF HUMORS

RHEITA

SCHICKARD

PICCOLOMINI

TYCHO

CLAVIUS

SOUTH

The Moon was formed billions of years ago. But no one is sure just how. Space was full of dust and rocks in those days, and these came together to form the Earth.

Perhaps when the Earth was first formed, a part of it broke loose and became the Moon.

Perhaps the dust and rocks came together in a whirling mass to form a large Earth and a smaller Moon at the same time.

The Moon is about 2,200 miles from side to side. This distance is called its diameter. The diameter of the Earth is about 8,000 miles, nearly four times as wide as the Moon.

The Earth is larger and much heavier, and so it pulls things toward itself more strongly. It has a stronger gravity, or gravitational pull. The Moon is caught in the Earth's gravitational pull. It moves around the Earth and can never get away. We say that the Moon is a satellite of the Earth.

You weigh so much because Earth's gravity pulls you. But the Moon's gravitational pull is only one-sixth as strong as the Earth's pull. If you weigh 96 pounds on the Earth, you would weigh only 16 pounds on the Moon.

You could jump high and far on the Moon because you would be so light. You could lift large rocks you couldn't move here on Earth.

Air and water are held to the Earth by gravity. The Moon's gravity is too weak to hold air and water. And so the Moon has no oceans, lakes, or rivers. It also has no air. It is an airless, very dry world.

The sounds we hear on Earth are carried by the air. There is no air on the Moon, so there is no sound.

People who go to the Moon must talk to each other by radio.

Dust in Earth's air scatters the sunlight. This makes Earth's daytime sky blue. The shadows are not completely dark.

But on the Moon, where there is no air, the sky is always black. You would be able to see stars there even in the daytime. Sunny places on the Moon would be very, very bright. But the shadows would be almost black.

Daytime on the Moon. A crescent Earth, the Sun and stars are in the sky.

Persons trying to live on the Moon would
have to wear space suits that would hold
air and protect them from heat and cold.

DURING THE DAYTIME
IN THE SUNLIGHT
212° F.

DURING THE NIGHTTIME
IN THE SHADOWS
−270° F.

The air on Earth is always moving. The
wind carries warmth from the hotter places to
the colder ones. For that reason it does not
get very hot or very cold on most of the Earth.

The Moon has no air or wind to carry the
Sun's heat. So it can get hot enough to boil
water in places on the Moon where the Sun is
shining straight down. And in the shadows,
it can get very much colder than it gets at
the South Pole on Earth.

The surface of the Moon has mountains in many places. But there are some plains, or flat places, too. The larger plains are called "seas" because long ago men thought there was water in them. They know better now.

The Moon has thousands of craters on it. Craters are something like small plains with circular walls around them. Some craters are only a few feet wide. Others are dozens of miles across. They may have been made when rocks from space smashed into the Moon.

Clavius, the largest crater on the Moon, is 146 miles wide. Tycho is easy to see. It is white, near the bottom of the Moon.

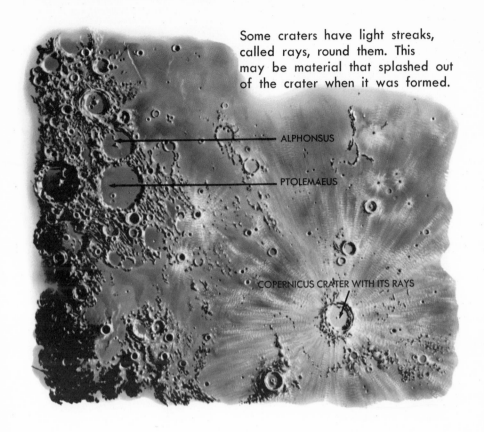

Some craters have light streaks, called rays, round them. This may be material that splashed out of the crater when it was formed.

ALPHONSUS

PTOLEMAEUS

COPERNICUS CRATER WITH ITS RAYS

It is possible that there were volcanoes on the Moon once. A few may still be hot underneath. Sometimes people at telescopes see clouds inside craters. Gas may still be appearing. Volcanoes in the past may also have made large cracks that are seen on the Moon. These are called rills.

11

The Moon turns on its axis
something like a ball would
turn on a spike. Here the
spike is the axis. The real
axis of the Moon cannot be
seen. It is an imaginary
line that goes through the
Moon from top to bottom.

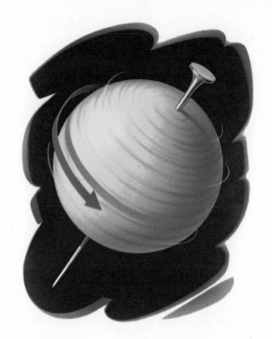

The Moon and the Earth are always moving.
They move in different ways. One way they
move is like a spinning top. This is called
turning about on the axis. The Earth rotates,
or turns about on its axis, once every 24 hours.
This time is called an Earth day.

The Moon takes longer to rotate once on
its axis. It takes a month of Earth time to
do it. The length of a "day" on the Moon
is 29 days and 13 hours of Earth time.

Other planets besides Earth have moons.
Some of these moons are larger than
ours, but most of them are smaller.

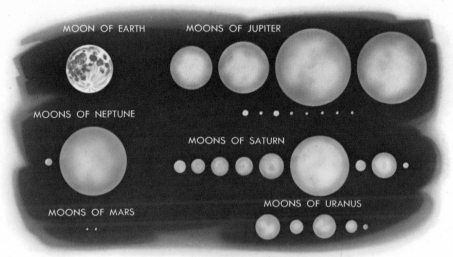

As the Moon turns on its axis, a man
standing on its surface would see the Sun and
stars rise and set. He would see that it takes
the Sun nearly 15 Earth days to seem to move
completely across the sky.

Daytime on the Moon is two weeks long.
Then there are two weeks of nighttime. Long
days and long nights are one reason why it
gets so hot on the Moon in its daytime and so
cold in its nighttime.

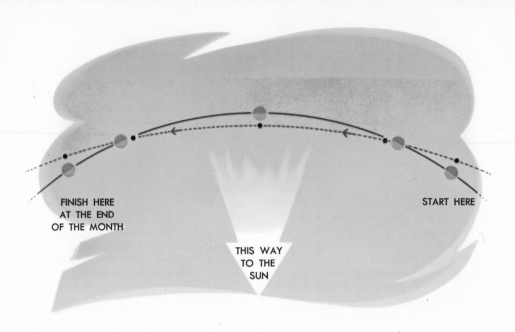

FINISH HERE
AT THE END
OF THE MONTH

START HERE

THIS WAY
TO THE
SUN

The Earth and the Moon travel this distance in one month. It takes the Earth and the Moon a year to make the whole trip around the Sun. The Moon travels around the Earth as it goes around the Sun.

The Earth and the Moon also move in another way. They go around the Sun together. The paths they follow are called orbits.

The gravitational pull of the Sun makes the Earth and the Moon move in their orbits. The picture shows how the Earth and Moon go around the Sun together.

14

The Earth's gravitational pull changes the Moon's orbit around the Sun. Look at the picture on page 14 again. See how the Moon seems to be going around the Earth. They are moving around the Sun from right to left.

If you could be in a space ship hovering high above the Earth's North Pole, you would see the Moon moving below you, going counterclockwise around the Earth. It would take about 27 days and 8 hours to go around the Earth once.

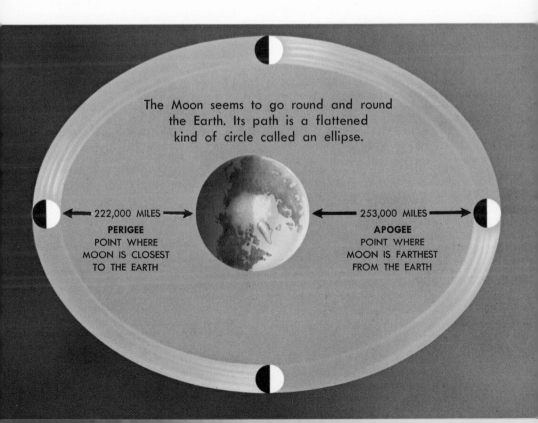

The Moon seems to go round and round the Earth. Its path is a flattened kind of circle called an ellipse.

←— 222,000 MILES —→

PERIGEE
POINT WHERE
MOON IS CLOSEST
TO THE EARTH

←— 253,000 MILES —→

APOGEE
POINT WHERE
MOON IS FARTHEST
FROM THE EARTH

It takes 27 days and 8 hours for the Moon to go once around the Earth. It takes exactly the same time for it to turn once about its own axis. The two kinds of turning match each other, so that the Moon always keeps the same side toward the Earth. Most of the other side cannot be seen by a person on the Earth.

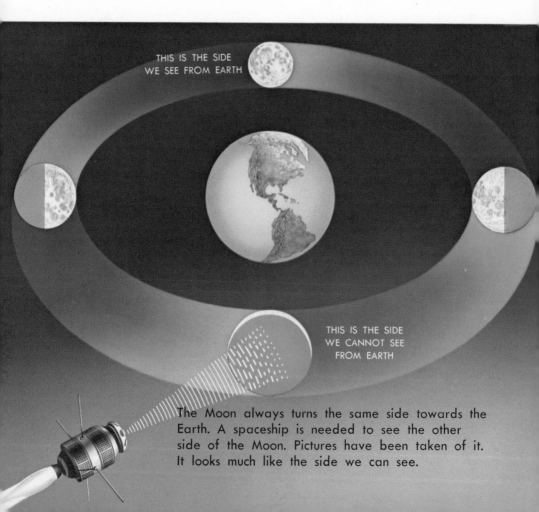

THIS IS THE SIDE
WE SEE FROM EARTH

THIS IS THE SIDE
WE CANNOT SEE
FROM EARTH

The Moon always turns the same side towards the Earth. A spaceship is needed to see the other side of the Moon. Pictures have been taken of it. It looks much like the side we can see.

The light from the Sun travels in straight lines. It lights up half of the Earth and Moon at a time.

EARTH

SUN

MOON

The Sun is a big ball of glowing gas. It gives off its own light. But the Moon is made of gray rock. It has no light of its own. It shines something like a mirror does. It reflects, or bounces back, the light it gets from the Sun.

Moonlight is sunlight that hits the Moon's surface and is reflected to us.

17

NEW MOON

If the sunlight could be blocked out, we might be able to see the new Moon. It would shine very faintly with the light reflected to it from the Earth.

The Moon is almost round, like a ball. But it seems to change its shape as the month goes by. This happens because of the way that sunlight shines on the Moon. The different-looking shapes are called the PHASES of the Moon.

When the Sun shines on the side of the Moon that is turned away from the Earth, we cannot see the Moon—even though it is still there. This is the time of the NEW MOON.

18

The Moon moves slowly around the Earth. The Sun shines partly on the side that is turned away from us and partly on the side turned toward us. Then we can see a narrow strip of sunlight like a curving fingernail shining on the Moon. We call this a CRESCENT MOON.

The crescent Moon seems to "set" in the sky a little after the Sun does. But this setting of the Moon is not a real movement. It seems to happen because of the way that the Earth rotates on its own axis.

The crescent Moon that comes a few days after the new Moon can only be seen at sunset. When the Sun rises in the morning, the crescent's light is "drowned" in the light of the bright Sun.

The Moon continues to move in its orbit. Sunlight shines over more and more of the side facing Earth. Seven days after the new Moon, half of the side facing us is lit up. This is called the Moon's FIRST QUARTER. Seven days after that, the whole Moon is lit up. This is called the FULL MOON. The full Moon rises at sunset and sets at sunrise.

When we see more than half of the Moon lighted up, it is called a gibbous Moon. You can see the gibbous Moon in the daytime.

The Earth reflects light from the Sun. We can see "earthshine" light up the Moon when the air is clear. This is called "the new Moon in the old Moon's arms."

The Moon moves on. Part of the sunlight slips past the edge of the full Moon to the other side. Seven days after the full Moon, we see the LAST QUARTER. Then we see a crescent Moon again. The "old" crescent rises in the morning a little before the Sun. Seven days after the last quarter, there will be a new Moon again. The Moon is once more not visible to us here on Earth.

21

The Moon goes completely around the Earth once every 27 days and 8 hours. The new Moon comes when the Sun shines behind the Moon.

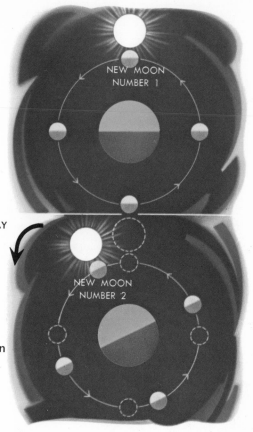

NEW MOON
NUMBER 1

THE SUN SEEMS
TO MOVE THIS WAY

But the Sun seems to move because of the way the Earth and Moon go around the Sun. So the Moon must travel TWO EXTRA DAYS EACH MONTH before it gets in front of the Sun again and the new Moon comes.

NEW MOON
NUMBER 2

It takes the Moon 27 days and 8 hours to make a complete turn about the Earth. But it takes about two days longer for it to go from one new Moon to the next. This happens because of the way that the Earth and Moon together move in their orbits around the Sun.

22

The time between one new Moon and another is 29 days and 13 hours. This period of time is called a lunar month, meaning "a month of the Moon." Long ago, people divided the year into twelve lunar months. This was their way of telling the seasons. The months we use in our calendar today are not lunar months. They have 28, 29, 30 or 31 days. But many calendars still tell us the days for the different phases of the Moon.

Some groups of people still tell time by the Moon's phases. Our word "month" comes from an old word meaning "Moon."

The Moon misses the Sun.
NO ECLIPSE OF THE SUN.

The Moon passes partly
in front of the Sun.
PARTIAL ECLIPSE OF THE SUN.

The Moon passes exactly
in front of the Sun.
TOTAL ECLIPSE OF THE SUN.

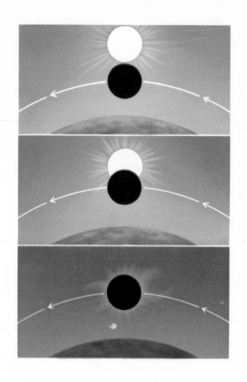

At each new Moon, the Moon passes between the Earth and the Sun. But it doesn't usually pass exactly between. It usually moves just a little above the Sun or a little below.

But sometimes the Moon passes exactly between the Earth and the Sun. Part of the light from the Sun is cut off by the passing Moon. This is called an ECLIPSE of the Sun.

24

We can think about an eclipse of the Sun in another way. Since sunlight cannot pass through the Moon, the Moon casts a shadow. The shadow is cone-shaped. It usually does not touch the Earth. But sometimes it moves across the Earth. When that happens, there is an eclipse. Inside of the small place where the shadow touches, people can see a total eclipse. There is darkness. In places that are near the shadow, people can see only a partial eclipse. Farther away from the shadow, people can see no eclipse at all.

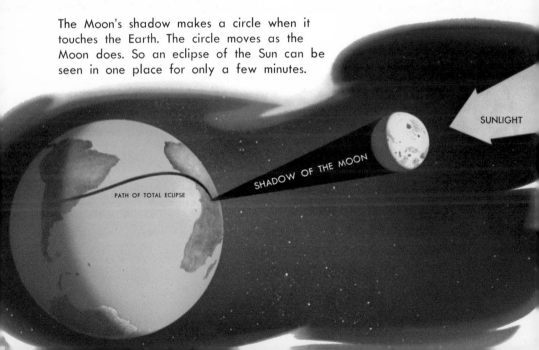

The Moon's shadow makes a circle when it touches the Earth. The circle moves as the Moon does. So an eclipse of the Sun can be seen in one place for only a few minutes.

SUNLIGHT

SHADOW OF THE MOON

PATH OF TOTAL ECLIPSE

Although the Moon and Sun seem to be nearly the same size, the Sun is really much bigger than the Moon. The Sun looks small because it is so far away.

Total eclipses of the Sun do not happen very often. Two to five are seen in different places on Earth every year. Astronomers travel long distances to be at places where a total eclipse will be seen. They can tell ahead of time just when and where the eclipse will be.

26

The Earth also makes a shadow in space. Sometimes this shadow touches the Moon. Then the full Moon grows darker as it passes through Earth's shadow. The Sun shining behind the Earth makes a red glow through Earth's air blanket. This reddish light shines on the Moon. Here on Earth, the Moon looks dark red. This is called an eclipse of the Moon.

The Earth's shadow is so wide that it sometimes takes the Moon as long as two hours to travel through it. There may be one or more eclipses of the Moon almost every year.

SUNLIGHT — EARTH'S SHADOW — MOON

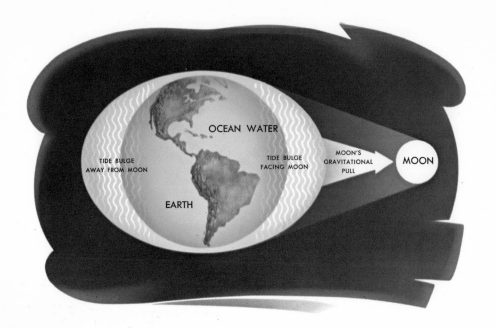

The Moon causes ocean tides.
The tide bulges are shown much
larger than they really are.

The Earth's gravity pulls on the Moon. The Moon's gravity pulls on the Earth, too. If the Earth were made of rubber, the Moon's gravitational pull would make it bulge.

The solid Earth holds together and hardly changes its shape at all because of the Moon's pull. But the water in the oceans does bulge.

The bulges are called tides.

The Earth turns around and around on its axis. But the ocean bulges stay in line with the Moon. The tide bulges seem to move around the Earth, so that the water rises and sinks on the shore. There will be a high tide and a low tide.

There are two ocean bulges, one on each side of the Earth, so there are two high tides and two low tides each day.

HIGH TIDE   LOW TIDE

The Moon lights up the night. It makes the sky beautiful. It causes eclipses of the Sun and makes the tides on the oceans. Long ago, people used the Moon's phases to mark the passing of a month of time.

Now men are exploring the Moon. It is a good thing that we have such a close neighbor in space. Space rockets can get to the Moon much more easily than they can get to the planets.

A space rocket can reach the Moon within a few days.

Words Younger Children May Need Help With

(Numbers refer to page on which the word first appears.)

5	billions		circular		counterclockwise
	whirling		dozens	**18**	phases
	diameter	**11**	volcanoes	**19**	crescent
	gravity		telescopes	**20**	quarter
	gravitational		rills	**23**	lunar
	satellite	**12**	axis		calendar
8	scatters		rotates	**24**	eclipse
	completely	**14**	orbits	**26**	astronomers
10	craters	**15**	hovering	**28**	tides

THINGS TO DO IN SCHOOL OR AT HOME

Observe the Moon. Look at the full Moon and compare it with the picture on page 4 of this book. How many of the seas and craters can you find? Look at the Moon again when it is in the first or last quarter. Are the seas and craters easier to observe at this time? Use field glasses or a small telescope to study the Moon. Rest your instrument against a tree, a chair, or some other firm surface and watch the Moon for several minutes. Why does the Moon drift out of sight when you hold the field glasses still?

Compare the time of moonrise. Does the weather section in your newspaper give the time of moonrise each day? Compare the times every day for a week. How much later does the Moon rise each night? Why is it impossible to see a crescent Moon at midnight?

See the optical illusion of a huge full Moon. The full Moon looks very large when it first rises. If you look at it later in the night, when it is high in the sky, it seems to have shrunk. Naturally the Moon stays the same size all the time. Its "changes" in size occur when our eyes play a trick on us. This is called an optical illusion. You can destroy the optical illusion and make the rising Moon look small by looking at it through a cardboard or paper tube with one eye while you keep the other eye shut.

Find out about Moon exploration. Collect pictures and articles about the human exploration of the Moon. Bring them to school and put them on the bulletin board, or make a scrapbook out of them. What good will it do for human beings to explore the Moon? Why would it be worthwhile to spend large sums of money in exploring the Moon? What will be needed for a permanent base of exploration on the Moon?

Study the tides. If you live near the ocean, watch the news every day for two weeks to see the times when high tide occurs. Note the position of the Moon in the sky at each high tide. Is the Moon always visible at high tide? Where is the Moon when you cannot see it at high tide time?

Read more about tides in an encyclopedia. What is a spring tide? What is a neap tide? During what phase of the Moon are the tides likely to be highest? Tides are most noticeable in large bodies of water such as the oceans. Smaller bodies of water have tides, too, but these may be so small that they are hardly visible. The Great Lakes have daily tides that rise and fall a few inches. If you live near a lake, you might try to measure it for tides. Find out when the new moon occurs. Measure the depth of the calm lake water in one spot at noon and again at the same spot at 6:00 P.M. If you are very careful and do your measuring when the water is flat calm, you may be able to find the tide in your lake.

Learn some of the legends and folklore about the Moon. There are many interesting folk tales about the Moon. Ask your librarian to help you find out about some of them. Do you know how we got the word "lunatic," meaning "insane"? Do you know anyone who believes that the phases of the Moon affect the weather or the number of fish that can be caught? Have you ever seen the Man in the Moon? Find out how Columbus obtained help from savage Indians by predicting an eclipse of the Moon.